KNIT COWLS

Add more color and texture to your wardrobe with easy-wearing cowls! These 10 patterns to knit were created by talented designer Lisa Gentry, and they use a wide variety of yarns ranging from light weight to super bulky weight. Besides being warm and attractive, cowls are your practical choice. They are seamed or knit into one continuous piece, or buttoned together for wearing. So while a scarf or muffler has loose ends that must be rewrapped or retied— once you put on a cowl, it stays put beautifully!

TABLE OF CONTENTS

LEISURE ARTS, INC.
Little Rock, Arkansas

garter ridge
COWL

Size: One size fits most

Finished Measurements:
17" wide x 21" circumference (43 cm x 53.5 cm)

MATERIALS

Super Bulky Weight Yarn **SUPER BULKY 6**
[6 ounces, 106 yards
(170 grams, 97 meters) per skein]:
Color A - 1 skein
Color B - 1 skein
Straight knitting needles, size 13 (9 mm) **or**
size needed for gauge
Yarn needle

GAUGE: In pattern,
8 sts = 4" (10 cm)
18 rows = 4¼" (10.75 cm)

BODY

With Color A, cast on 34 sts.

Row 1 (Right side)**:** Knit across.

Rows 2-4: Purl across.

Row 5: Knit across.

Rows 6 and 7: Purl across.

Row 8: Knit across.

Rows 9 and 10: Purl across.

Rows 11-13: Knit across.

Row 14: Purl across.

Rows 15 and 16: Knit across.

Row 17: Purl across.

Row 18: Knit across.

Rows 19-45: Repeat Rows 1-18 once, then repeat Rows 1-9 once **more**.

Rows 46-54: Cut Color A; with Color B, repeat Rows 10-18.

Rows 55-90: Repeat Rows 1-18 twice.

Bind off all sts in **knit**, leaving a long end for sewing.

Thread yarn needle with long end. Fold Body in half, matching cast on edge to bound off edge; weave edges together (**Fig.** 18, *page* 35).

shoulder fringed
COWL

Size: One size fits most

Finished Measurements:
4³/₄" wide x 19¹/₂" circumference (buttoned)
(12 cm x 49.5 cm)

MATERIALS

Super Bulky Weight Yarn **SUPER BULKY 6**
[3.5 ounces, 52 yards
(100 grams, 47 meters) per skein]:
  2 skeins
Straight knitting needles, size 15 (10 mm) **or**
  size needed for gauge
Crochet hook, size K (6.5 mm) for fringe
1¹/₄" (32 mm) Button
Sewing needle and matching thread

GAUGE: In pattern,
          10 sts and 14 rows = 4³/₄" (12 cm)

Techniques used:
• YO (**Fig. 5b**, pages 32 & 33)
• P2 tog (**Fig. 17**, page 35)

BODY
Cast on 10 sts.

Row 1 (Right side): Knit across.

Row 2: K2, P6, K2.

Rows 3-5: Repeat Rows 1 and 2 once, then repeat
Row 1 once **more**.

Row 6 (Buttonhole row): K2, P2, [YO, P2 tog
(**buttonhole made**)], P2, K2.

Repeat Rows 1 and 2 for pattern until piece
measures approximately 24¹/₂" (62 cm) from cast on
edge, ending by working Row 2.

Bind off all sts in **knit**.

FRINGE
Cut a piece of cardboard 4" wide (10 cm) and 5"
long (12.5 cm). Wind the yarn loosely and evenly
lengthwise around the cardboard until the card is
filled, then cut across one end. Repeat until you
have approximately 50 lengths.
Fold one length in half. With **wrong** side of long
edge of Body facing and bound off edge to your
right, insert hook in end of bind off row and draw the
folded end up through st; pull loose ends through
the folded end (**Fig. 1a**); draw the knot up tightly
(**Fig. 1b**).
Repeat in every other row across long edge, then in
each st along cast on edge.
Lay Cowl flat on a hard surface and trim ends evenly.

Fig. 1a

Fig. 1b

With **right** side facing, center button approximately
2¹/₂" (6.5 cm) from bound off edge and sew in place.

buttoned lace
COWL

Size: One size fits most

Finished Measurements:
Width - 8³/₄" (22 cm)
Neck circumference (buttoned) - 18" (45.5 cm)
Bottom circumference (buttoned) - 29" (73.5 cm)

MATERIALS
Light Weight Yarn **③** LIGHT
[5 ounces, 459 yards
(141 grams, 420 meters) per skein]:
one skein
24" (61 cm) Circular knitting needle,
size 6 (4 mm) **or** size needed for gauge
Markers
1" (25 mm) Buttons - 4
Sewing needle and matching thread

GAUGE: In pattern,
one repeat (11 sts) = 2¹/₂" (6.25 cm);
30 rows = 4" (10 cm)

Techniques used:
• YO (**Fig.** 5a, *pages* 32 & 33)
• Knit increase (**Figs.** 6a & b, *page* 33)
• Purl increase (**Fig.** 7, *page* 33)
• M2 (**Figs.** 9a & b, *page* 33)
• K2 tog (**Fig.** 10, *page* 34)
• Slip 1 as if to **knit**, K1, PSSO (**Figs.** 15a & b, *page* 35)
• Slip 1 as if to **knit**, K2 tog, PSSO (**Figs.** 16a & b, *page* 35)

RIBBING
Cast on 126 sts.

Rows 1-7: (K1, P1) across.

Row 8 (Buttonhole row)**:** (K1, P1) 5 times **(button band)**, place marker (*see Markers, page* 32), (K1, P1) across to last 12 sts, place marker, (K1, P1) twice, [slip 1 as if to **knit**, K1, PSSO, YO (buttonhole)], (K1, P1) 3 times **(buttonhole band)**.

Rows 9 and 10: (K1, P1) across.

Row 11 (Increase row)**:** (K1, P1) across to next marker, (K1, P1) across to next marker increasing 8 sts evenly spaced, (K1, P1) across: 134 sts (112 sts between markers).

BODY

Row 1 (Right side)**:** (K1, P1) across to next marker, K1, K2 tog, K5, YO, K1, YO, K2, ★ slip 1 as if to **knit**, K2 tog, PSSO, K5, YO, K1, YO, K2; repeat from ★ across to within 2 sts of next marker, slip 1 as if to **knit**, K1, PSSO, (K1, P1) across.

Row 2: (K1, P1) across to next marker, purl across to next marker, (K1, P1) across.

Row 3: (K1, P1) across to next marker, K1, K2 tog, K4, YO, K3, YO, K1, ★ slip 1 as if to **knit**, K2 tog, PSSO, K4, YO, K3, YO, K1; repeat from ★ across to within 2 sts of next marker, slip 1 as if to **knit**, K1, PSSO, (K1, P1) across.

Row 4: (K1, P1) across to next marker, purl across to next marker, (K1, P1) across.

Row 5: (K1, P1) across to next marker, K1, K2 tog, K3, YO, K5, YO, ★ slip 1 as if to **knit**, K2 tog, PSSO, K3, YO, K5, YO; repeat from ★ across to within 2 sts of next marker, slip 1 as if to **knit**, K1, PSSO, (K1, P1) across.

Row 6: (K1, P1) across to next marker, purl across to next marker, (K1, P1) across.

Row 7 (Increase row)**:** (K1, P1) across to next marker, K1, K2 tog, K2, YO, K1, YO, K5, ★ slip 1 as if to **knit**, K2 tog, PSSO, K2, YO, K1, YO, K5; repeat from ★ across to within 2 sts of next marker, slip 1 as if to **knit**, K1, PSSO, slip marker, M2, (K1, P1) across: 136 sts (112 sts remain between markers).

Row 8: (K1, P1) across to next marker, purl across to next marker, (K1, P1) across.

Row 9: (K1, P1) across to next marker, K1, K2 tog, K1, YO, K3, YO, K4, ★ slip 1 as if to **knit**, K2 tog, PSSO, K1, YO, K3, YO, K4; repeat from ★ across to within 2 sts of next marker, slip 1 as if to **knit**, K1, PSSO, (K1, P1) across.

Row 10: (K1, P1) across to next marker, purl across to next marker, (K1, P1) across.

Row 11: (K1, P1) across to next marker, K1, K2 tog, YO, K5, YO, K3, ★ slip 1 as if to **knit**, K2 tog, PSSO, YO, K5, YO, K3; repeat from ★ across to within 2 sts of next marker, slip 1 as if to **knit**, K1, PSSO, (K1, P1) across.

Row 12: (K1, P1) across to next marker, purl across to next marker, (K1, P1) across.

Row 13 (Increase and Buttonhole row): (K1, P1) across to next marker, K1, K2 tog, K5, YO, K1, YO, K2, ★ slip 1 as if to **knit**, K2 tog, PSSO, K5, YO, K1, YO, K2; repeat from ★ across to within 2 sts of next marker, slip 1 as if to **knit**, K1, PSSO, slip marker, M2, (K1, P1) 4 times, [slip 1 as if to **knit**, K1, PSSO, YO (**buttonhole**)], (K1, P1) 3 times: 138 sts (112 sts remain between markers).

Rows 14-24: Repeat Rows 2-12: 140 sts (112 sts remain between markers).

Row 25 (Increase row): (K1, P1) across to next marker, K1, K2 tog, K5, YO, K1, YO, K2, ★ slip 1 as if to **knit**, K2 tog, PSSO, K5, YO, K1, YO, K2; repeat from ★ across to within 2 sts of next marker, slip 1 as if to **knit**, K1, PSSO, slip marker, M2, (K1, P1) across: 142 sts (112 sts remain between markers).

Rows 26-28: Repeat Rows 2-4.

Row 29 (Buttonhole row): (K1, P1) across to next marker, K1, K2 tog, K3, YO, K5, YO, ★ slip 1 as if to **knit**, K2 tog, PSSO, K3, YO, K5, YO; repeat from ★ across to within 2 sts of next marker, slip 1 as if to **knit**, K1, PSSO, (K1, P1) 6 times, [slip 1 as if to **knit**, K1, PSSO, YO (**buttonhole**)], (K1, P1) 3 times.

Rows 30-36: Repeat Rows 6-12: 144 sts (112 sts remain between markers).

Row 37 (Increase row): (K1, P1) across to next marker, K1, K2 tog, K5, YO, K1, YO, K2, ★ slip 1 as if to **knit**, K2 tog, PSSO, K5, YO, K1, YO, K2; repeat from ★ across to within 2 sts of next marker, slip 1 as if to **knit**, K1, PSSO, slip marker, M2, (K1, P1) across: 146 sts (112 sts remain between markers).

Rows 38-44: Repeat Rows 2-8: 148 sts (112 sts remain between markers).

Row 45 (Buttonhole row): (K1, P1) across to next marker, K1, K2 tog, K1, YO, K3, YO, K4, ★ slip 1 as if to **knit**, K2 tog, PSSO, K1, YO, K3, YO, K4; repeat from ★ across to within 2 sts of next marker, slip 1 as if to **knit**, K1, PSSO, (K1, P1) 9 times, [slip 1 as if to **knit**, K1, PSSO, YO (**buttonhole**)], (K1, P1) 3 times.

Rows 46-48: Repeat Rows 10-12.

Rows 49-54: Repeat Rows 1-6.

Bind off all sts loosely in ribbing across bands and in knit across center sts.

Sew buttons to button band opposite buttonholes.

squiggles and a flower
COWL

Size: One size fits most

Finished Measurements:
10" wide x 25" circumference (25.5 cm x 63.5 cm)

MATERIALS
Medium Weight Yarn **4** MEDIUM
[3.5 ounces, 170 yards
(100 grams, 156 meters) per skein]:
   2 skeins
29" (73.5 cm) Circular knitting needle,
   size 9 (5.5 mm) **or** size needed for gauge
Marker
⅞" (22 mm) Button
Yarn needle
Sewing needle and matching thread

GAUGE: In pattern (slightly stretched),
   one repeat (12 sts) = 2¾" (7 cm)
   and 8 rnds = 1¼" (3.25 cm)

Techniques used:
- K1 tbl (**Fig.** 4, *page* 32)
- YO (**Figs.** 5a & b, *pages* 32 & 33)
- Knit increase (**Figs.** 6a & b, *page* 33)
- K2 tog (**Fig.** 10, *page* 34)
- K3 tog (**Fig.** 12, *page* 34)
- Slip 1 as if to **knit**, K2 tog, PSSO (**Figs.** 16a & b, *page* 35)

Rnd 5: (K1, YO) twice, slip 1 as if to **knit**, K2 tog, PSSO, P3, K3 tog, ★ YO, (K1, YO) 3 times, slip 1 as if to **knit**, K2 tog, PSSO, P3, K3 tog; repeat from ★ around to last st, YO, K1, YO.

Rnds 6-8: K5, P3, (K9, P3) around to last 4 sts, K4.

Rnds 9-64: Repeat Rnds 1-8, 7 times.

Bind off all sts in **knit**.

BAND

Cast on 8 sts.

Knit every row until piece measures approximately 1" (2.5 cm) from cast on edge.

Buttonhole Row: K3, bind off next 2 sts, knit across: 3 sts on each side of bind off.

Next Row: K3, YO twice, K3: 8 sts.

Next Row: K4, K1 tbl, K3.

Knit every row until Band measures approximately 10" (25.5 cm) from cast on edge.

Bind off all sts in **knit**.

Center button approximately ½" (12 mm) from bound off edge and sew in place.

BODY

Cast on 108 sts; being careful **not** to twist the cast on, place a marker to indicate the beginning of the rnd (*see Markers & Circular Knitting, page 32*).

Rnd 1 (Right side)**:** P2, K3 tog, YO, (K1, YO) 3 times, slip 1 as if to **knit**, K2 tog, PSSO, ★ P3, K3 tog, YO, (K1, YO) 3 times, slip 1 as if to **knit**, K2 tog, PSSO; repeat from ★ around to last st, P1.

Rnds 2-4: P2, K9, (P3, K9) around to last st, P1.

FLOWER

Cast on 9 sts.

Row 1 (Right side)**:** Knit across.

Row 2: P1, (YO, P1) across: 17 sts.

Row 3: K1, (knit increase, K1) across: 25 sts.

Row 4: Knit across.

Row 5: ★ Chain 8 (Figs. 2a-c), K1, pass first st on right needle over second st leaving one st on needle, slip st from right needle back onto left needle; repeat from ★ across; cut yarn leaving a long end for sewing, pull end through last st to secure.

Thread yarn needle with long end. With **right** side together and end of rows matching, sew end of rows together, leaving cast on edge open.

Wrap the Band around the cowl; insert the button through the buttonhole on the Band and then through the center hole of the Flower.

CHAINING WITH A NEEDLE

K1 (counts as first chain, now and throughout), ★ insert the left needle through the **front** of the stitch on the right needle (Fig. 2a), yarn over the right needle (Fig. 2b), pull the yarn through the stitch on the right needle, drop the stitch off the left needle (Fig. 2c); repeat from ★ as many times as indicated in the instructions.

Fig. 2a

Fig. 2b

Fig. 2c

button as you please
COWL

Size: One size fits most

Finished Measurements:
   6" wide x 28" long (15 cm x 71 cm)

MATERIALS
   Bulky Weight Yarn **BULKY 5**
   [3 ounces, 135 yards
   (85 grams, 123 meters) per skein]:
      One skein
   Straight knitting needles,
      size 9 (5.5 mm) **or** size needed for gauge
   1" (25 mm) Buttons - 2
   Sewing needle and matching thread

GAUGE: In pattern,
      1 repeat (7 sts) = $1^{3}/_{4}$" (4.5 cm)
      16 rows = 4" (10 cm)

Techniques used:
- YO (*Figs. 5a-d, pages* 32 & 33)
- K2 tog (*Fig.* 10, *page* 34)
- Slip 1 as if to **knit**, K2 tog, PSSO (*Figs. 16a & b, page* 35)

BODY
Cast on 25 sts.

Row 1 (Right side)**:** K1, P1, ★ YO, K2, slip 1 as if to **knit**, K2 tog, PSSO, K2; repeat from ★ 2 times **more**, P1, K1: 22 sts.

Row 2: P1, K1, (YO, P6) 3 times, K1, P1: 25 sts.

Repeat Rows 1 and 2 for pattern until Body measures approximately 28" (71 cm) from cast on edge, ending by working Row 2.

Bind off all sts in **knit**.

With **right** side facing and using photo as a guide for placement, sew buttons $^{1}/_{2}$" (12 mm) from bound off edge. Use yarn over spaces to button cowl.

tempting texture
COWL

Size: One size fits most

Finished Measurements:
17" wide x 32" circumference (43 cm x 81.5 cm)

MATERIALS
Medium Weight Yarn **4** MEDIUM
[3.5 ounces, 210 yards
(100 grams, 192 meters) per skein]:
  3 skeins
29" (73.5 cm) Circular knitting needle,
  size 8 (5 mm) **or** size needed for gauge
Marker

GAUGE: In pattern,
  one repeat (17 sts) = 4" (10 cm)
  and Rnds 5-13 = 1½" (3.75 cm)

Techniques used:
- YO (**Fig. 5a, pages 32 & 33**)
- K2 tog (**Fig. 10, page 34**)
- Slip 1 as if to **knit**, K1, PSSO (**Figs. 15a & b, page 35**)

BODY
Cast on 136 sts; being careful **not** to twist the cast on, place a marker to indicate the beginning of the rnd (*see Markers & Circular needles, page 32*).

Rnd 1 (Right side)**:** Knit around.

Rnd 2: Purl around.

Rnds 3 and 4: Repeat Rnds 1 and 2.

Rnd 5: Knit around.

Rnd 6: ★ K2 tog 3 times, YO, (K1, YO) 5 times, (slip 1 as if to **knit**, K1, PSSO) 3 times; repeat from ★ around.

Rnds 7-10: Knit around.

Rnds 11-13: Purl around.

Rnds 14-103: Repeat Rnds 5-13, 10 times.

Bind off all sts in **purl**.

rose neck wrap
COWL

Size: One size fits most

Finished Measurements:
 6³/₄" wide x 29" long (17 cm x 73.5 cm)

MATERIALS
 Medium Weight Yarn
 [3.5 ounces, 205 yards
 (100 grams, 187 meters) per skein]:
  2 skeins
 24"-29" (61-73.5 cm) Circular knitting
  needles, sizes 7 (4.5 mm) **and** 8 (5 mm) **or**
  sizes needed for gauge
 1¹/₂" (38 mm) Pin back

GAUGE: With smaller size needles,
  in Stockinette Stitch,
  20 sts and 26 rows = 4" (10 cm)

Techniques used:
- K1 tbl (**Fig. 4**, *page 32*)
- YO (**Fig. 5a**, *pages 32 & 33*)
- M1 (**Figs. 8a & b**, *page 33*)
- K2 tog (**Fig. 10**, *page 34*)
- Slip 1 as if to **knit**, K1, PSSO (**Figs. 15a & b**, *page 35*)

BOTTOM RIBBING
With larger size circular knitting needle,
cast on 135 sts.

Row 1: P3, (K1, P3) across.

Row 2 (Right side): K3, (P1, K3) across.

Repeat Rows 1 and 2 for pattern until Bottom
Ribbing measures 1¹/₂" (4 cm), ending by working
Row 1.

BODY

Change to smaller size circular knitting needle.

Rows 1-4: Knit across.

Row 5 (Increase row)**:** Knit across working 54 M1 increases evenly spaced: 189 sts.

Row 6: Purl across.

Row 7: ★ K1, YO, K3, K2 tog, slip 1 as if to **knit**, K1, PSSO, K3, YO; repeat from ★ across to last 2 sts, K2.

Row 8: Purl across.

Row 9: K2, ★ YO, K3, K2 tog, slip 1 as if to **knit**, K1, PSSO, K3, YO, K1; repeat from ★ across.

Row 10: Purl across.

Row 11: ★ K1, YO, K3, K2 tog, slip 1 as if to **knit**, K1, PSSO, K3, YO; repeat from ★ across to last 2 sts, K2.

Row 12: Purl across.

Row 13 (Decrease row)**:** Knit across decreasing 54 sts evenly spaced: 135 sts.

Row 14: Purl across.

Rows 15-18: Knit across.

Rows 19-32: Repeat Rows 5-18.

TOP RIBBING

Change to larger size circular knitting needle.

Row 1 (Right side)**:** K3, (P1, K3) across.

Row 2: P3, (K1, P3) across.

Repeat Rows 1 and 2 until Top Ribbing measures 1¾" (4.5 cm), ending by working Row 2.

Bind off all sts in **knit**.

FLOWER

With larger size circular knitting needle, cast on 5 sts.

Row 1: K4, (K in front, K in back, K in front, K in back, K in front) **all** in next st: 9 sts.

Row 2 (Right side)**:** P5, with yarn forward, slip 1 as if to **purl**, with yarn back, slip st from right needle back to left needle (5 sts on right needle); **turn**.

Row 3: K5.

Rows 4 and 5: Repeat Rows 2 and 3.

Row 6: P5, pass second, third, fourth and fifth st on right needle over first st (leaving one st on right needle), P4: 5 sts.

Rows 7-120: Repeat Rows 1-6, 19 times: 5 sts.

Bind off remaining sts in **knit**.

Roll straight edge to form a spiral and sew in place. Sew to pin back and pin to cowl.

diamonds with a twist
COWL

Size: One size fits most

Finished Measurements:
   9" wide x 52" circumference (23 cm x 132 cm)

MATERIALS
   Medium Weight Yarn
   [3 ounces, 131 yards
   (85 grams, 121 meters) per skein]:
      3 skeins
   29" (73.5 cm) Circular knitting needle,
      size 9 (5.5 mm) **or** size needed for gauge
   Marker

GAUGE: In pattern,
   2 repeats (18 sts) = 4³/₄" (12 cm)
   2 repeats (16 rnds) = 2¹/₂" (6.25 cm)

BODY
Cast on 198 sts; twist the cast on sts **once**, place marker to indicate the beginning of the rnd (*see Markers & Circular Knitting, page 32*).

Rnd 1: K4, P1, (K8, P1) around to last 4 sts, K4.

Rnd 2: K3, P3, (K6, P3) around to last 3 sts, K3.

Rnd 3: K2, P5, (K4, P5) around to last 2 sts, K2.

Rnd 4: K1, P7, (K2, P7) around to last st, K1.

Rnd 5: Purl around.

Rnd 6: K1, P7, (K2, P7) around to last st, K1.

Rnd 7: K2, P5, (K4, P5) around to last 2 sts, K2.

Rnd 8: K3, P3, (K6, P3) around to last 3 sts, K3.

Rnds 9-57: Repeat Rnds 1-8, 6 times; then repeat Rnd 1 once **more**.

Bind off all sts in **knit**.

lace with a twist
COWL

Size: One size fits most

Finished Measurements:
   7" wide x 46$\frac{1}{2}$" circumference (18 cm x 118 cm)

MATERIALS
   Medium Weight Yarn [MEDIUM 4]
   [2.5 ounces, 153 yards
   (70 grams, 140 meters) per skein]:
   2 skeins
   Straight knitting needles, size 10 (6 mm)
   or size needed for gauge
   Yarn needle

GAUGE: In Stockinette Stitch,
         16 sts and 18 rows = 3$\frac{1}{2}$" (9 cm)

Techniques used:
• YO (*Figs. 5c & d, page* 33)
• K2 tog (*Fig.* 10, *page* 34)
• K4 tog (*Fig.* 14, *page* 34)

BODY
Cast on 33 sts.

Row 1: K4 (Edging), (P6, YO, K2 tog) 3 times, P1, K4 (Edging).

Row 2: K5, P2, (K6, P2) twice, K 10.

Row 3: K4, (P5, YO, K2 tog, K1) 3 times, P1, K4.

Row 4: (K5, P3) 3 times, K9.

Row 5: K4, (P4, YO, K2 tog, K2) 3 times, P1, K4.

Row 6: K5, P4, (K4, P4) twice, K8.

Row 7: K4 tog, (P3, YO, K2 tog, K3) 3 times, P1, K4 tog: 27 sts.

Row 8: (K, P, K, P) **all** in first st, K1, (P5, K3) 3 times, (K, P, K, P) **all** in last st: 33 sts.

Row 9: K4, (P2, YO, K2 tog, K4) 3 times, P1, K4.

Row 10: K5, P6, (K2, P6) twice, K6.

Row 11: K4, P1, (YO, K2 tog, K5, P1) 3 times, K4.

Row 12: K5, P7, (K1, P7) twice, K5.

Row 13: K4, P1, (K5, K2 tog, YO, P1) 3 times, K4.

Row 14: K5, P7, (K1, P7) twice, K5.

Row 15: K4 tog, P1, (K4, K2 tog, YO, P2) 3 times, K4 tog: 27 sts.

Row 16: (K, P, K, P) **all** in first st, (K2, P6) 3 times, K1, (K, P, K, P) **all** in last st: 33 sts.

Row 17: K4, P1, (K3, K2 tog, YO, P3) 3 times, K4.

Row 18: K7, P5, (K3, P5) twice, K5.

Row 19: K4, P1, (K2, K2 tog, YO, P4) 3 times, K4.

Row 20: K8, P4, (K4, P4) twice, K5.

Row 21: K4, P1, (K1, K2 tog, YO, P5) 3 times, K4.

Row 22: K9, (P3, K5) 3 times.

Row 23: K4 tog, P1, (K2 tog, YO, P6) 3 times, K4 tog: 27 sts.

Row 24: (K, P, K, P) **all** in first st, (K6, P2) 3 times, K1, (K, P, K, P) **all** in last st: 33 sts.

Rows 25-240: Repeat Rows 1-24, 9 times.

Bind off all sts in pattern.

Thread yarn needle with long end. Fold Body in half, bringing short edges together and flip one short edge over once creating a twist. Weave short edges together (**Fig. 18,** *page* 35).

sideways made
COWL

Size: One size fits most

Finished Measurements:
12" wide (at point) x 40" long (30.5 cm x 101.5 cm)

MATERIALS
Medium Weight Yarn
[4 ounces, 186 yards
(113 grams, 170 meters) per skein]:
  2 skeins
Straight knitting needles,
  size 9 (5.5 mm) **or** size needed for gauge
Marker

GAUGE: In Garter Stitch,
  17 sts and 32 rows = 4" (10 cm)

Techniques used:
• YO (**Fig.** 5a, *pages 32 & 33*)
• Knit increase (**Figs.** 6a & b, *page 33*)
• M1 (**Figs.** 8a & b, *page 33*)
• K2 tog (**Fig.** 10, *page 34*)
• K2 tog tbl (**Fig.** 11, *page 34*)
• K3 tog tbl (**Fig.** 13, *page 34*)
• P2 tog (**Fig.** 17, *page 35*)

BODY
Beginning at the side point of the triangle, cast on 3 sts.

Row 1 (Right side)**:** K2, knit increase: 4 sts.

Row 2: Knit increase, K1, place marker (*see Markers, page* 32), K2: 5 sts.

Row 3: K1, M1, K1, slip marker, YO, K3: 7 sts.

Row 4: Knit across.

Row 5: K3, slip marker, YO, K4: 8 sts.

Row 6: Knit across.

Row 7: K2, M1, K1, slip marker, YO, knit across: 10 sts.

Row 8: Knit across.

Row 9: Knit across to marker, slip marker, YO, knit across: 11 sts.

Row 10: Knit across.

Row 11: K3, M1, K1, slip marker, YO, knit across: 13 sts.

Row 12: Knit across.

Row 13: Knit across to marker, slip marker, YO, knit across: 14 sts.

Row 14: Bind off 4 sts, knit across: 10 sts.

Row 15: K4, M1, K1, slip marker, (YO, K1) 5 times: 16 sts.

Row 16: YO, knit across: 17 sts.

Row 17: Knit across to marker, slip marker, YO, knit across: 18 sts.

Row 18: Knit across.

Row 19: K5, M1, K1, slip marker, YO, knit across: 20 sts.

Row 20: Bind off 6 sts, knit across: 14 sts.

Row 21: Knit across to marker, slip marker, YO, K1, (YO twice, K2 tog) 3 times: 18 sts.

Row 22: YO, K2, (P1, K2) 3 times, slip marker, knit across: 19 sts.

Row 23: K6, M1, K1, slip marker, YO, knit across: 21 sts.

Row 24: Knit across.

Row 25: Knit across to marker, slip marker, YO, knit across: 22 sts.

Row 26: Bind off 6 sts, knit across: 16 sts.

Row 27: K7, M1, K1, slip marker, YO, K1, (YO twice, K2 tog) 3 times, K1: 21 sts.

Row 28: YO, K3, (P1, K2) 3 times, slip marker, knit across: 22 sts.

Row 29: Knit across to marker, slip marker, YO, knit across: 23 sts.

Row 30: Knit across.

Row 31: K8, M1, K1, slip marker, YO, knit across: 25 sts.

Row 32: Bind off 6 sts, knit across: 19 sts.

Row 33: Knit across to marker, slip marker, YO, K1, (YO twice, K2 tog) 4 times: 24 sts.

Row 34: YO, K2, (P1, K2) 4 times, slip marker, knit across: 25 sts.

Row 35: Knit across to within one st of marker, M1, K1, slip marker, YO, K2 tog tbl, knit across: 26 sts.

Row 36: Knit across.

Row 37: Knit across to marker, slip marker, YO, knit across: 27 sts.

Row 38: Bind off 6 sts, knit across: 21 sts.

Row 39: Knit across to within one st of marker, M1, K1, slip marker, YO, K2 tog tbl, (YO twice, K2 tog) 4 times: 26 sts.

Row 40: YO, K2, (P1, K2) 4 times, slip marker, knit across: 27 sts.

Row 41: Knit across to marker, slip marker, YO, K2 tog tbl, knit across.

Row 42: Knit across.

Row 43: Knit across to within one st of marker, M1, K1, slip marker, YO, knit across: 29 sts.

Row 44: Bind off 6 sts, knit across: 23 sts.

Row 45: Knit across to marker, slip marker, YO, K2 tog tbl, (YO twice, K2 tog) 4 times: 27 sts.

Row 46: YO, K2, (P1, K2) 4 times, slip marker, knit across: 28 sts.

Rows 47-142: Repeat Rows 35-46, 8 times: 52 sts.

Row 143: Knit across to within 3 sts of marker, K2 tog, K1, slip marker, YO, K2 tog tbl, knit across: 51 sts.

Row 144: Knit across.

Row 145: Knit across to marker, slip marker, YO, knit across: 52 sts.

Row 146: Bind off 6 sts, knit across: 46 sts.

Row 147: Knit across to within 3 sts of marker, K2 tog, K1, slip marker, YO, K2 tog tbl, (YO twice, K2 tog) 4 times: 49 sts.

Row 148: YO, K2, (P1, K2) 4 times, slip marker, knit across: 50 sts.

Row 149: Knit across to marker, slip marker, YO, K2 tog tbl, knit across.

Row 150: Knit across.

Row 151: Knit across to within 3 sts of marker, K2 tog, K1, slip marker, YO, knit across.

Row 152: Bind off 6 sts, knit across: 44 sts.

Row 153: Knit across to marker, slip marker, YO, K2 tog tbl, (YO twice, K2 tog) 4 times: 48 sts.

Row 154: YO, K2, (P1, K2) 4 times, slip marker, knit across: 49 sts.

Rows 155-250: Repeat Rows 143-154, 8 times: 25 sts.

Row 251: Knit across to within 3 sts of marker, K2 tog, K1, slip marker, YO, K2 tog tbl, knit across: 24 sts.

Row 252: Knit across.

Row 253: Knit across to marker, slip marker, YO, K3 tog tbl, knit across: 23 sts.

Row 254: Bind off 6 sts, knit across: 17 sts.

Row 255: Knit across to within 3 sts of marker, K2 tog, K1, slip marker, YO, K2 tog tbl, (YO twice, K2 tog) 3 times: 19 sts.

Row 256: YO, K2, (P1, K2) 3 times, slip marker, knit across: 20 sts.

Row 257: Knit across to marker, slip marker, YO, knit across: 21 sts.

Row 258: Knit across.

Row 259: Knit across to within 3 sts of marker, K2 tog, K1, slip marker, YO, knit across.

Row 260: Bind off 6 sts, knit across: 15 sts.

Row 261: Knit across to marker, slip marker, YO, K2 tog tbl, (YO, K2 tog) 3 times.

Row 262: YO, knit across: 16 sts.

Row 263: K4, K2 tog, K1, slip marker, YO, knit across.

Row 264: Knit across.

Row 265: Knit across to marker, slip marker, YO, knit across: 17 sts.

Row 266: Bind off 6 sts, knit across: 11 sts.

Row 267: K3, K2 tog, K1, slip marker, YO, K2 tog tbl, (YO, K1) 3 times: 13 sts.

Row 268: YO, knit across: 14 sts.

Row 269: Knit across to marker, slip marker, YO, K2 tog tbl, knit across.

Row 270: Knit across.

Row 271: K2, K2 tog, K1, slip marker, YO, K3 tog tbl, knit across: 12 sts.

Row 272: Knit across.

Row 273: Knit across to marker, slip marker, YO, K3 tog tbl, knit across: 11 sts.

Row 274: Knit across.

Row 275: K1, K2 tog, K1, slip marker, YO, K3 tog tbl, knit across: 9 sts.

Row 276: K3, P2 tog, K4: 8 sts.

Row 277: Knit across to marker, slip marker, YO, K3 tog tbl, K2: 7 sts.

Row 278: K1, P2 tog, K4: 6 sts.

Row 279: K1, K2 tog, YO, K3 tog tbl: 4 sts.

Row 280: Knit across.

Bind off remaining sts in **knit**.

general instructions

ABBREVIATIONS

cm	centimeters
K	knit
M1	Make 1
M2	Make 2
mm	millimeters
P	purl
PSSO	pass slipped stitch over
Rnd(s)	round(s)
st(s)	stitch(es)
tbl	through back loop
tog	together
YO	yarn over

SYMBOLS & TERMS

★ — work instructions following ★ as many **more** times as indicated in addition to the first time.

( ) or [ ] — work enclosed instructions **as many** times as specified by the number immediately following **or** work all enclosed instructions in the stitch indicated **or** contains explanatory remarks.

colon (:) — the number(s) given after a colon at the end of a row or round denote(s) the number of stitches you should have on that row or round.

GAUGE

Exact gauge is essential for proper size. Before beginning your Cowl, make a sample swatch using the yarn and needles specified in the individual instructions. After completing the swatch, measure it, counting your stitches and rows or rounds carefully. If your swatch is larger or smaller than specified, **make another, changing needle size to get the correct gauge.** Keep trying until you find the size needles that will give you the specified gauge.

KNIT TERMINOLOGY	
UNITED STATES	**INTERNATIONAL**
gauge =	tension
bind off =	cast off
yarn over (YO) =	yarn forward (yfwd) **or** yarn around needle (yrn)

Yarn Weight Symbol & Names	LACE 0	SUPER FINE 1	FINE 2	LIGHT 3	MEDIUM 4	BULKY 5	SUPER BULKY 6
Type of Yarns in Category	Fingering, size 10 crochet thread	Sock, Fingering, Baby	Sport, Baby	DK, Light Worsted	Worsted, Afghan, Aran	Chunky, Craft, Rug	Bulky, Roving
Knit Gauge Range* in Stockinette St to 4" (10 cm)	33-40** sts	27-32 sts	23-26 sts	21-24 sts	16-20 sts	12-15 sts	6-11 sts
Advised Needle Size Range	000-1	1 to 3	3 to 5	5 to 7	7 to 9	9 to 11	11 and larger

*GUIDELINES ONLY: The chart above reflects the most commonly used gauges and needle sizes for specific yarn categories.

** Lace weight yarns are usually knitted on larger needles to create lacy openwork patterns. Accordingly, a gauge range is difficult to determine. Always follow the gauge stated in your pattern.

■□□□ BEGINNER	Projects for first-time knitters using basic knit and purl stitches. Minimal shaping.
■■□□ EASY	Projects using basic stitches, repetitive stitch patterns, simple color changes, and simple shaping and finishing.
■■■□ INTERMEDIATE	Projects with a variety of stitches, such as basic cables and lace, simple intarsia, double-pointed needles and knitting in the round needle techniques, mid-level shaping and finishing.
■■■■ EXPERIENCED	Projects using advanced techniques and stitches, such as short rows, fair isle, more intricate intarsia, cables, lace patterns, and numerous color changes.

KNITTING NEEDLES																			
U.S.	0	1	2	3	4	5	6	7	8	9	10	10½	11	13	15	17	19	35	50
U.K.	13	12	11	10	9	8	7	6	5	4	3	2	1	00	000	---	---	---	---
Metric - mm	2	2.25	2.75	3.25	3.5	3.75	4	4.5	5	5.5	6	6.5	8	9	10	12.75	15	19	25

MARKERS

As a convenience to you, we have used markers to help distinguish the beginning of a round or a pattern. Place markers as instructed. You may use purchased markers or tie a length of contrasting color yarn around the needle.

When you reach a marker on a row or round, slip it from the left needle tip to the right needle tip; remove it when no longer needed.

CIRCULAR KNITTING

When you knit in **rounds**, you are going to work around on the outside of the circle, with the **right** side of the knitting facing you.

Cast on the number of stitches indicated. Make sure that the cast on ridge lays on the inside of the needle and never rolls around the needle (**Fig. 3**), unless the instructions specify otherwise as for the Diamond With A Twist Cowl, page 22, or Lace With A Twist Cowl, page 24.

Hold the needle so that the ball of yarn is attached to the stitch closest to the right hand point. Place a marker on the right hand point to mark the beginning of the rounds (*see Markers*). Knit the stitches on the left hand point.

Fig. 3

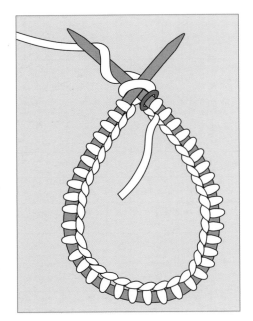

KNIT ONE THROUGH BACK LOOP
(*abbreviated* K1 *tbl*)

To knit through the back loop, with yarn in back, insert right needle into back of the stitch (**Fig. 4**).

Fig. 4

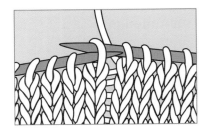

YARN OVERS

A yarn over (*abbreviated* YO) is simply placing the yarn over the right needle creating an extra stitch. Since the yarn over produces a hole in the knit fabric, it is used for a lacy effect. On the row following a yarn over, you must be careful to keep it on the needle and treat it as a stitch by knitting or purling it as instructed.

To make a yarn over, you'll loop the yarn over the needle like you would to knit or purl a stitch, bringing it either to the front or to the back of the piece so that it'll be ready to work the next stitch, creating a new stitch on the needle as follows:

After a knit stitch, before a knit stitch
Bring the yarn forward **between** the needles, then back **over** the top of the right-hand needle, so that it is now in position to **knit** the next stitch (**Fig. 5a**).

After a purl stitch, before a purl stitch
Take the yarn **over** the right-hand needle to the back, then forward **under** it, so that it is now in position to **purl** the next stitch (**Fig. 5b**).

After a knit stitch, before a purl stitch
Bring the yarn forward **between** the needles, then back **over** the top of the right-hand needle and forward **between** the needles again, so that it is now in position to **purl** the next stitch (**Fig. 5c**).

After a purl stitch, before a knit stitch
Take the yarn **over** the right-hand needle to the back, so that it is now in position to **knit** the next stitch (**Fig. 5d**).

Fig. 5a

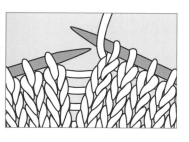

Fig. 5b

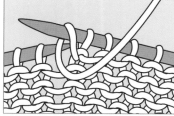

Fig. 5c

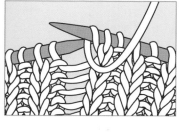

Fig. 5d

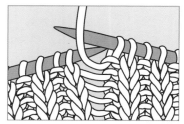

INCREASES
KNIT INCREASE

Knit the next stitch but do **not** slip the old stitch off the left needle (**Fig. 6a**). Insert the right needle into the **back** loop of the **same** stitch and knit it (**Fig. 6b**), then slip the old stitch off the left needle.

Fig. 6a

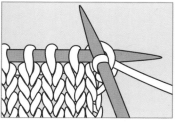

Fig. 6b

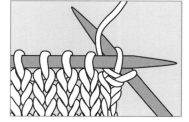

PURL INCREASE

Purl the next stitch but do **not** slip the old stitch off the left needle. Insert the right needle into the back loop of the **same** stitch from **back** to **front** (**Fig. 7**) and purl it. Slip the old stitch off the left needle.

Fig. 7

MAKE ONE (*abbreviated* M1)

Insert the **left** needle under the horizontal strand between the stitches from the **front** (**Fig. 8a**), then knit into the **back** of the strand (**Fig. 8b**).

Fig. 8a

Fig. 8b

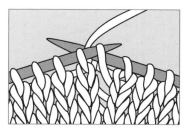

MAKE TWO (*abbreviated* M2)

Insert the **left** needle under the horizontal strand between the stitches from the **back** (**Fig. 9a**), then knit into the **front** of the stitch (**Fig. 9b**) but do **not** slip the stitch off the left needle. Insert the **right** needle into the **back** loop of the **same** stitch and knit it, then slip the old stitch off the left needle.

Fig. 9a

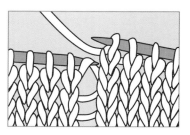

Fig. 9b

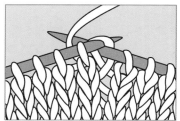

33

DECREASES

KNIT 2 TOGETHER (abbreviated K2 tog)

Insert the right needle into the **front** of the first two stitches on the left needle as if to **knit** (**Fig.** 10), then **knit** them together as if they were one stitch.

Fig. 10

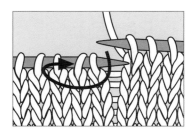

KNIT 2 TOGETHER THROUGH BACK LOOP (abbreviated K2 tog tbl)

Insert the right needle into the **back** loop of the first two stitches on the left needle (**Fig.** 11), then **knit** them together as if they were one stitch.

Fig. 11

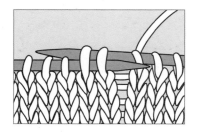

KNIT 3 TOGETHER (abbreviated K3 tog)

Insert the right needle into the **front** of the first three stitches on the left needle as if to **knit** (**Fig.** 12), then **knit** them together as if they were one stitch.

Fig. 12

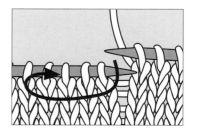

KNIT 3 TOGETHER THROUGH BACK LOOP (abbreviated K3 tog tbl)

Insert the right needle into the **back** loop of the first three stitches on the left needle (**Fig.** 13), then **knit** them together as if they were one stitch.

Fig. 13

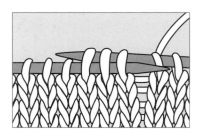

KNIT 4 TOGETHER (abbreviated K4 tog)

Insert the right needle into the **front** of the first four stitches on the left needle as if to **knit** (**Fig.** 14), then **knit** them together as if they were one stitch.

Fig. 14

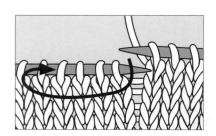

SLIP 1, KNIT 1, PASS SLIPPED STITCH OVER (abbreviated slip 1, K1, PSSO)

Slip one stitch as if to **knit** (**Fig. 15a**). Knit the next stitch. With the left needle, bring the slipped stitch over the knit stitch (**Fig. 15b**) and off the needle.

Fig. 15a   **Fig. 15b**

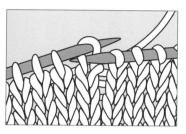 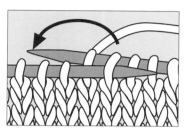

SLIP 1, KNIT 2 TOGETHER, PASS SLIPPED STITCH OVER
(abbreviated slip 1, K2 tog, PSSO)

Slip one stitch as if to **knit** (**Fig. 16a**), then knit the next two stitches together (**Fig. 10, page 34**). With the left needle, bring the slipped stitch over the stitch just made (**Fig. 16b**) and off the needle.

Fig. 16a   **Fig. 16b**

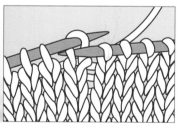 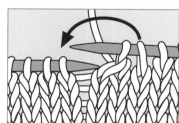

PURL 2 TOGETHER (abbreviated P2 tog)

Insert the right needle into the **front** of the first two stitches on the left needle as if to **purl** (**Fig. 17**), then **purl** them together as if they were one stitch.

Fig. 17

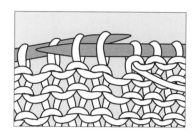

WEAVING SEAMS

Seams that are joined by weaving appear seamless. With **right** side facing you and the edges even, bring the needle from behind the work and through the center of the first stitch, leaving a long end to be woven in later. ★ Bring the needle over the top of the seam and pick up both loops of the corresponding stitch on the second side (**Fig. 18**). Bring the needle back over the seam and pick up the inverted V of the next stitch. Repeat from ★ across. Pull the yarn gently every 2 or 3 stitches, being careful to maintain even tension.

Fig. 18

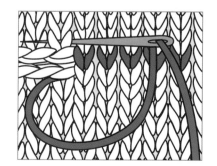

yarn information

The Cowls in this leaflet were made using various weights of yarn. Any brand of the specified weight of yarn may be used. It is best to refer to the yardage/meters when determining how many balls or skeins to purchase. Remember, to arrive at the finished size, it is the GAUGE/TENSION that is important, not the brand of yarn. For your convenience, listed below are the specific yarns used to create our photography models.

GARTER RIDGE COWL
Lion Brand® Wool-Ease® Thick & Quick®
Color A - #146 Fig
Color B - #103 Blossom

SHOULDER FRINGED COWL
Bernat® Colorama
#05335 Forget Me Not

BUTTONED LACE COWL
Lion Brand® Babysoft®
#099 Cream

SQUIGGLES AND A FLOWER COWL
Lion Brand® Vanna's Choice®
#108 Dusty Blue

BUTTON AS YOU PLEASE COWL
Lion Brand® Jiffy®
#173 Grass Green

TEMPTING TEXTURE COWL
Patons® Classic Wool
#77010 Natural Marl

ROSE NECK WRAP COWL
Patons® Canadiana
#10443 Pale Currant

DIAMONDS WITH A TWIST COWL
Stitch Nation by Debbie Stoller™ Alpaca Love™
#3920 Ruby

LACE WITH A TWIST COWL
Red Heart® Boutique™ Midnight™
#1944 Harvest Moon

SIDEWAYS MADE COWL
Red Heart® Eco-Ways™
#3422 Yam

PRODUCTION TEAM:
Technical Writer/Editor - Linda A. Daley and Cathy Hardy
Editorial Writer - Susan McManus Johnson
Senior Graphic Artist - Lora Puls
Graphic Artists - Becca Snider and Dana Vaughn
Photo Stylist - Angela Alexander
Photographers - Jason Masters and Ken West